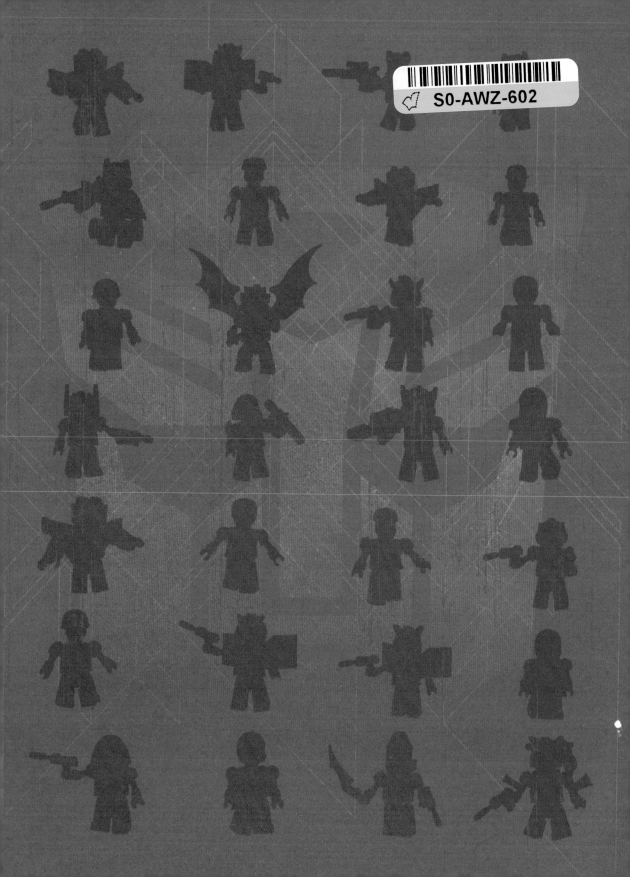

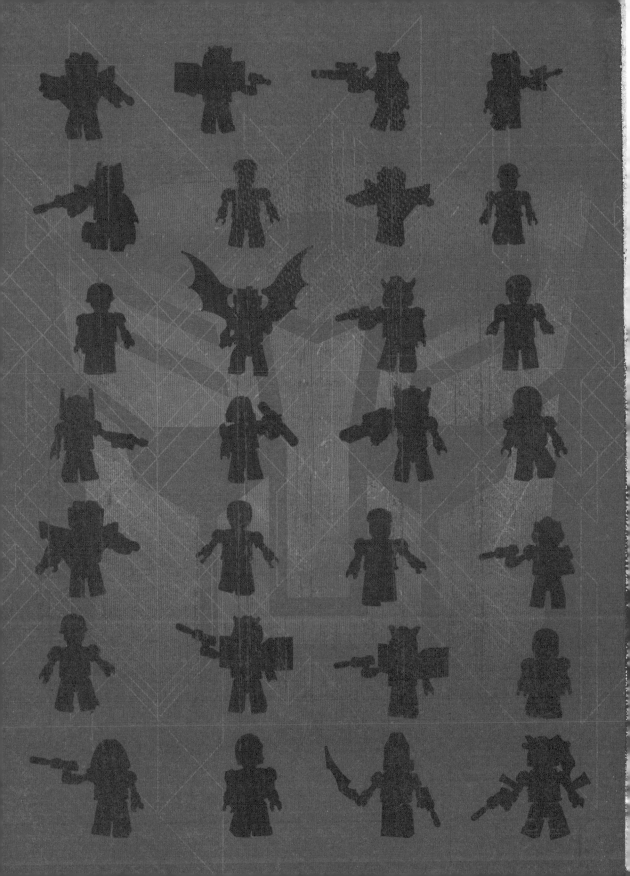

KRE-O
TRANSFORMERS
CHARACTER ENCYCLOPEDIA

KRE-O TRANSFORMERS CHARACTER ENCYCLOPEDIA

By Brandon T. Snider

Little, Brown and Company

New York • Boston

CONTENTS

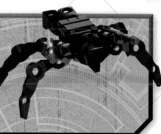

Introduction

Inside this book you'll find your favorite characters and discover new ones! Each figure featured has an item number (IN), product name (PN), and piece count (PC) listed under its name. Use the handy checklists at the end of each section to keep track of your KREON collection as it grows! Figures are not shown to scale.

2011: BATTLE FOR EARTH

Sentinel Prime

IN: 30687   PN: SENTINEL PRIME   PC: 386

ALLIANCE: Autobot

STRENGTH: Wisdom

BIO: Once the clever and merciful leader of the Aut... ...s his days fishing i...

1"

1.75"

Item Number

Piece Count

Product Name

Average KREON Height: 1.75 in/44.5 mm

Orion Pax

IN: **SPECIAL EDITION**   PN: **ORION PAX**   PC: **N/A**

ALLIANCE: Autobot

STRENGTH: Intelligence

BIO: Orion Pax never imagined the adventures he'd see when he was back filing books on Cybertron. The future Prime once had a quiet and simple life. Now he spends his time space-bridging to battles separated by light-years.

THE BIG RACE

VROOOM!

The race begins...

This is all me!

As Bumblebee and Megatron enter a tunnel...

Starscream waits on the other side.

I'll fix his wagon, all right.

VROOOM!

VROOOM!

He tries to take out Bumblebee...

...but he hits the wrong bot!

Oh no!

Curse that jet!

FINISH!

HOORAY!!!

BATTLE FOR EARTH: 2011 FIGURES

The Autobots and Decepticons waged war against each other for centuries, ravaging their home world of Cybertron. In an effort to spread even more destruction, the Decepticons traveled the cosmos looking for new worlds to conquer and ended up on Earth. The Autobots soon followed and have since made the planet their home. Their mission: to protect the KREON citizens from the Decepticons and bring their enemies to justice. It's not easy, but some bots have got to do it.

11

ALLIANCE: Autobot

STRENGTH: Leadership

BIO: Optimus Prime doesn't take guff from *anyone*! As the dedicated leader of the Autobots, Optimus is committed to protecting Earth from the evil grasp of the Decepticons. One of these days he'll get around to retiring, but for now he fights for what's right!

Mirage

IN: 31145   PN: MIRAGE   PC: 119

ALLIANCE: Autobot

STRENGTH: Covert operations

BIO: When the Autobots need a super-spy to infiltrate the Decepticons' ranks, they call on Mirage. And if things get too hot, Mirage can always use his slick Energon-infused tires to hightail it out of there. Hopefully just in time to crack open some Energon and watch the KRE-O Grand Prix.

Jazz

IN: 31146   PN: **AUTOBOT JAZZ**   PC: 122

ALLIANCE: Autobot

STRENGTH: Hand-to-hand combat

BIO: Jazz is always itching for a fight. The thing that *really* gets him pumped for battle is his favorite song "Nothin' but a Bot Thing"! He also loves relaxing ringside at a boxing match and enjoying a nice demolition derby.

Ratchet

IN: 30662   PN: **AUTOBOT RATCHET**   PC: 187

ALLIANCE: Autobot

STRENGTH: Mechanics

BIO: Ratchet's mechanical skills are world renowned, but he doesn't work for free. If you want something done well, you'll have to pay. That is, unless you throw a spider at him. Then he'll just run away.

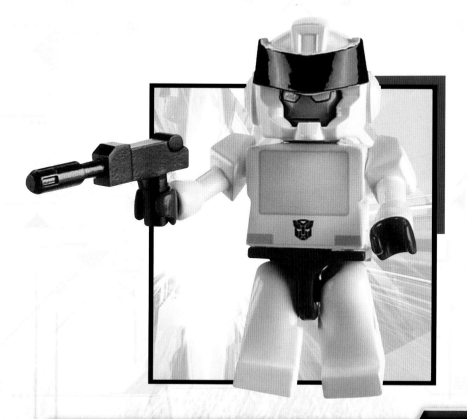

Prowl

IN: 30690   PN: PROWL   PC: 174

ALLIANCE: Autobot

STRENGTH: Computation

BIO: Prowl is always in the corner fiddling around with his calculator and doing smart stuff. Logic and intelligence really fire up Prowl's circuits! One day he hopes to follow in the footsteps of his idol, cybercop Block Samson. An Autobot can dream, can't he?

Sideswipe

IN: 31771   PN: SIDESWIPE   PC: 220

ALLIANCE: Autobot

STRENGTH: Swordsmanship

BIO: Sideswipe is the Autobots' chief weapons master and unofficial head of swashbuckling. He's a total genius with a blade and has been known to slice and dice his way through a Decepticon or two. Don't bother him while he's sharpening his swords! He can be a little bit of a cranky-pants.

Red Alert

IN: 36421   PN: BUMBLEBEE   PC: 335

ALLIANCE: Autobot

STRENGTH: Security

BIO: Red Alert can be a little overprotective of his Autobot comrades, but it's because he's extremely focused on doing his job as head of security. He greatly values logic and reason, which sometimes makes him hard to deal with. Maybe the poor guy should loosen his thrusters a little?

Bumblebee

IN: 36421   PN: BUMBLEBEE   PC: 335

ALLIANCE: Autobot

STRENGTH: Combat

BIO: Bumblebee is an unstoppable party machine who loves playing pranks on his unsuspecting Autobot buddies. And if there's a human party around, he'll crash it and stay till the break of dawn (or at least until he has to fight again). That's just how he rolls.

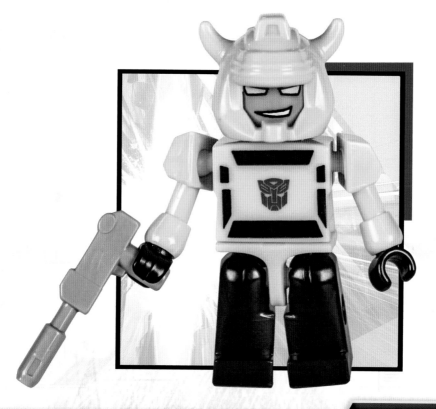

 Sentinel Prime

IN: 30687 PN: SENTINEL PRIME PC: 386

ALLIANCE: Autobot

STRENGTH: Wisdom

BIO: Once the clever and merciful leader of the Autobots, Sentinel Prime now spends his days fishing in the many bountiful bodies of water Earth has to offer. Since passing on the reins of leadership, Sentinel Prime uses his free time to reflect on his greatest triumphs. He also loves a good nap.

Blue Streak

IN: 30689   PN: OPTIMUS PRIME   PC: 542

ALLIANCE: Autobot

STRENGTH: Chattering

BIO: Whether he's in combat or at a birthday party, Blue Streak will talk an Autobot's audio circuits off! His friends know he means well, but Blue Streak's constant yammering can be pretty distracting on the battlefield. Thankfully, good ol' Optimus Prime can muzzle him when it's time to fight.

Starscream

IN: 30667   PN: STARSCREAM   PC: 316

ALLIANCE: Decepticon

STRENGTH: Aerial assault

BIO: Did you hear that Starscream thinks he's a better leader than Megatron? Of course you did, because *it's all he talks about*! The Decepticons might actually win their war with the Autobots if Starscream spent more time doing his *job* instead of whining. Just kidding!

ALLIANCE: Decepticon

STRENGTH: Computation

BIO: Everyone knows that Shockwave is a master at solving the most difficult mathematical equations. What people *don't* know is that he has been taking hip-hop dance classes in his spare time and hopes to perform professionally! But first he needs to find the perfect outfit.

Megatron

IN: 30688   PN: MEGATRON   PC: 310

ALLIANCE: Decepticon

STRENGTH: Subjugation

BIO: Most people think Megatron is a grouchy jerk who lives to annihilate the Autobots. His closest friends know that inside that evil robotic body he's really just a softy who enjoys good television. Oh, and *destruction*! He *loves* that.

Thundercracker

IN: 30687   PN: SENTINEL PRIME   PC: 386

ALLIANCE: Decepticon

STRENGTH: Aerial acrobatics

BIO: Enemies beware: The sky is Thundercracker's domain! Just as long as you don't count birds and all the other stuff that flies. He often mocks his land-bound colleagues behind their backs but is careful not to draw the wrath of Megatron in the process.

Soundwave

IN: 30687   PN: SENTINEL PRIME   PC: 386

ALLIANCE: Decepticon

STRENGTH: Communications

BIO: Soundwave doesn't have much of a personality, but he's a loyal and reliable Decepticon...for now. Who knows what he's plotting in those circuits of his? His motto should be "Speak softly and carry a gigantic laser pistol."

ALLIANCE: Decepticon

STRENGTH: Teleportation

BIO: Skywarp is a dim-witted Decepticon who does and says anything that Megatron tells him to. He also has a mischievous streak and loves to play pranks on his Decepticon buddies. His favorite prank is called the Oil Slick Surprise! It's pretty *crude*.

Checklist

AUTOBOTS

- ☐ Optimus Prime
- ☐ Mirage
- ☐ Jazz
- ☐ Ratchet
- ☐ Prowl
- ☐ Sideswipe
- ☐ Red Alert
- ☐ Bumblebee
- ☐ Sentinel Prime
- ☐ Blue Streak

DECEPTICONS

- ☐ **Starscream**
- ☐ **Shockwave**
- ☐ **Megatron**
- ☐ **Thundercracker**
- ☐ **Soundwave**
- ☐ **Skywarp**

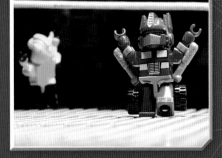

The reigning champs!

...versus Megatron?!

BOOM!!!

GASP!

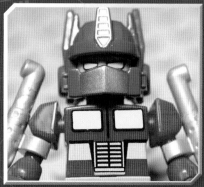

BATTLE FOR ENERGON: 2012 FIGURES

The Decepticons grew impatient during their time on Earth and quickly resorted to dangerous and violent means to secure Energon, the source of their power. They began a varied assault, but thankfully their plans were derailed by the heroic Autobots and their KREON allies, who together were able to restore a sense of order. However, Energon resources continue to dwindle, and the Decepticons have grown increasingly desperate.

33

Ironhide

IN: 36951   PN: DESTRUCTION SITE DEVASTATOR   PC: 560

ALLIANCE: Autobot

STRENGTH: Patrolling

BIO: There's no one Optimus Prime trusts more in battle than his old friend Ironhide. His parts might be a little rusty and he can't change modes as quickly as he used to, but he can still shoot an Omega Black Hole Cannon pretty well. He'll even tell you all about it! Over and over again. Until you lose your mind.

Trooper

IN: 36954   PN: CYCLE CHASE   PC: 75

ALLIANCE: Autobot

STRENGTH: Freedom fighting

BIO: Autobot troopers always stand proud and are ready for battle at a moment's notice. They're loyal, hardworking, and committed to fighting for what's right. Don't let them catch you stealing; they *really* hate thieves!

Cliffjumper

IN: 38781   PN: DECEPTICON AMBUSH   PC: 80

ALLIANCE: Autobot

STRENGTH: Hand-to-hand combat

BIO: Don't compare Cliffjumper to his Autobot buddies. He really hates that. As the team's most spontaneous and unpredictable member, Cliffjumper goes out of his way to show everyone how unique he really is. He loves a good disguise and delights in showing off his mad skills in battle.

Energon Mode

Wheeljack

IN: 38771   PN: STREET SHOWDOWN   PC: 273

ALLIANCE: Autobot

STRENGTH: Inventing

BIO: You won't find a more committed Autobot than Wheeljack. He's been dreaming up new and awesome weapons to use against the Decepticons. He's famous for creating the Quantum Circuit Breaker, but don't mention it around Ratchet because he'll get jealous.

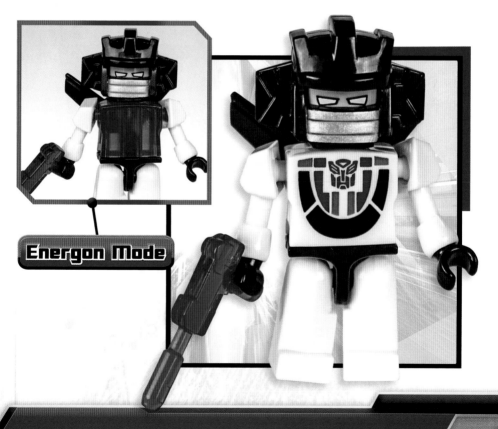

Energon Mode

Optimus Prime

IN: 98812   PN: BATTLE FOR ENERGON   PC: 379

ALLIANCE: Autobot

STRENGTH: Leadership

BIO: Optimus Prime has shown great maturity and restraint as the leader of the Autobots. But when Megatron and the Decepticons began their dark quest for Energon, he assembled his best bots and quickly took down his enemies. Oh, and have you seen him dance? Optimus has some moves!

Energon Mode

Bumblebee

IN: 98814   PN: STEALTH BUMBLEBEE   PC: 257

ALLIANCE: Autobot

STRENGTH: Combat

BIO: There isn't a bot in this universe that can beat Bumblebee in a drag race. He *lives* to burn rubber! He's so slick and quick that he makes the Decepticons look like a bunch of robo-turkeys. Sure, he loves to show off his sweet moves, but who wouldn't when you're the coolest Autobot ever?

Energon Mode

ALLIANCE: Decepticon

STRENGTH: Destruction

BIO: Devastator is a brutal Decepticon who annihilates everything in his path, leaving mass destruction in his wake. Oh, and he also loves destroying anything he considers weak and unworthy. Not a nice guy, really.

Energon Mode

Barricade

IN: 36954   PN: CYCLE CHASE   PC: 75

ALLIANCE: Decepticon

STRENGTH: Bullying

BIO: Barricade is a merciless and violent maniac who does *whatever* he wants, *whenever* he wants, *wherever* he wants! He thinks of himself as vastly superior to his fellow Decepticons and loves showing off. He is positively savage in his quest to acquire Energon to power his dark weaponry.

Energon Mode

Vehicon

IN: 38781   PN: DECEPTICON AMBUSH   PC: 80

ALLIANCE: Decepticon

STRENGTH: Compliance

BIO: If there's one thing that Megatron values in his soldiers, it's obedience. Vehicon always shows up on time, never deviates from the plan, and always keeps his mouth shut. What more can an evil leader ask for?

Knock Out

IN: 38771   PN: **STREET SHOWDOWN**   PC: 273

ALLIANCE: Decepticon

STRENGTH: Weaponry

BIO: Knock Out loves sweet-talking his fellow Decepticons into letting him experiment on them. Who doesn't love a good upgrade? He enjoys watching his evil creations wreak havoc upon the Autobots. Knock Out may seem like a cold guy, but there's one thing he loves more than anything: himself!

Megatron

IN: 98812   PN: BATTLE FOR ENERGON   PC: 379

ALLIANCE: Decepticon

STRENGTH: Subjugation

BIO: Megatron is completely consumed with his quest for Energon, and nothing will stand in his way. Nothing! Oh, except maybe the fact that his Decepticon cronies keep messing things up for him. Seriously, why does he hire so many dummies?

Energon Mode

Vortex

IN: 36959   PN: ROTOR RAGE   PC: 217

ALLIANCE: Decepticon

STRENGTH: Flying

BIO: Vortex is known to have a few loose screws in that evil head of his. When he's not scraping together all the Energon he can find (he loves that stuff!), he's taking unsuspecting Autobots on crazy helicopter rides to their doom. Be careful with this wild bot or you might end up in trouble.

Energon Mode

Checklist

AUTOBOTS

- [ ] Ironhide
- [ ] Trooper
- [ ] Cliffjumper
- [ ] Wheeljack
- [ ] Optimus Prime
- [ ] Bumblebee

How YOU doin'?

DECEPTICONS

- ☐ **Constructicon Devastator**
- ☐ **Barricade**
- ☐ **Vehicon**
- ☐ **Knock Out**
- ☐ **Megatron**
- ☐ **Vortex**

QUEST FOR ENERGON

PART I

At the bank...

ENERGON MOVED TO CITY BANK!

MICRO-CHANGER BOTS BAFFLE SCIENTISTS!

Hello, I'd like to take out a loan...

Outside the bank, construction vehicles combine to form Devastator.

Devastator takes the roof off the bank!

While Devastator keeps the Autobots busy, the Decepticons steal the Energon!

TO BE CONTINUED...

BEAST HUNTERS: 2013 FIGURES

For a period of time, the Autobots and Decepticons were able to put aside their differences and decrease their hostilities for the sake of the KREONS, but all of that changed when the Predacons were unleashed. This ancient breed of beastly robots wasted no time annihilating everything in their path. The extent of the Predacons' alliance with the Decepticons is currently unknown, but anyone attempting to engage either group should do so with extreme caution.

53

Windcharger

IN: A2205   PN: MECH VENOM STRIKE   PC: 49

ALLIANCE: Autobot

STRENGTH: Speed

BIO: Windcharger is a quick-thinking Autobot with lightning-fast reflexes. He loves showing off in combat, especially when he's fighting Corhada, a beastly Predacon enemy. Windcharger tires easily and occasionally sneaks out of battle to get a nice refreshing glass of Energon.

Trailcutter

IN: A2205   PN: DRAGON ASSAULT   PC: 42

ALLIANCE: Autobot

STRENGTH: Social consciousness

BIO: While most Autobots dream of kicking major Decepticon booty, Trailcutter favors the peaceful approach. Sadly it's an approach that doesn't always work out—but at least he *tries*. It's all for the best because he'd rather just sit in a tree and stare at the sky all day anyway. Oh, to be in nature!

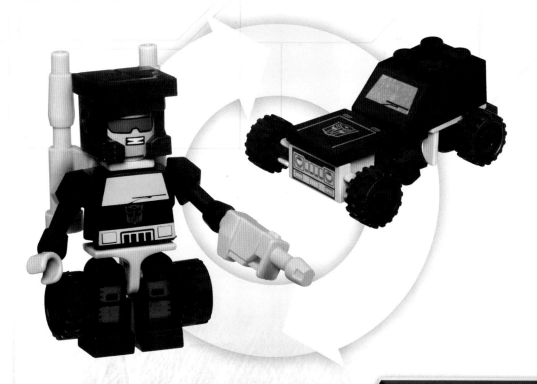

Optimus Prime

IN: **A2203**   PN: **BEAST BLADE OPTIMUS PRIME**   PC: **251**

ALLIANCE: Autobot

STRENGTH: Leadership

BIO: Optimus has a sweet sword! Enough said.

Bumblebee

IN: A2202   PN: BATTLE NET BUMBLEBEE   PC: 178

ALLIANCE: Autobot

STRENGTH: Combat

BIO: Who has no thumbs and a new weapon? This guy.

Ratchet

IN: A5412 PN: AUTOBOT COMMAND CENTER PC: 461

ALLIANCE: Autobot

STRENGTH: Mechanics

BIO: Ratchet is an Autobot with eclectic tastes. After a long day of repairing his Autobot pals, he loves to relax by reading about all the hot new hood ornaments. And on the weekends you might just find him cruising curio shops for vintage KRE-O bricks.

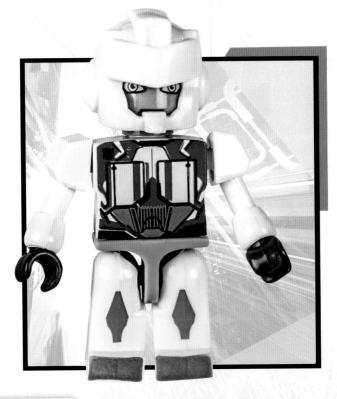

Arcee

IN: **A5412**   PN: **AUTOBOT COMMAND CENTER**   PC: **461**

ALLIANCE: Autobot

STRENGTH: Sharpshooting

BIO: Arcee is an excellent sniper and one of Optimus Prime's most trusted officers. She's quick on the draw, and her aim is perfect. Many Decepticons had to find that out the hard way. When danger threatens the people of Earth, she's always first in the line of defense!

Bumblebee

IN: A5412   PN: AUTOBOT COMMAND CENTER   PC: 461

ALLIANCE: Autobot

STRENGTH: Combat

BIO: He may seem like a fun-loving party dude, but when it's time to get serious, Bumblebee can always buckle down and focus. He takes pride in defending and protecting his fellow KREONS while stationed in the new Autobot Command Center. It's also a good place for Optimus Prime to keep an eye on him, but don't tell Bumblebee that!

Shockwave

IN: **A5412** PN: **AUTOBOT COMMAND CENTER** PC: **461**

ALLIANCE: Decepticon

STRENGTH: Computation

BIO: Shockwave is cold, calculating, and logical. These are all traits that make him a merciless Decepticon warrior. That is, unless you turn on the song "Shake Your Bot-Bot." It's his favorite.

Ripclaw

IN: **A2201**   PN: **RIPCLAW STRIKE**   PC: **199**

ALLIANCE: Predacon

STRENGTH: Aviation

BIO: Ripclaw's savage nature fits perfectly in line with his fellow Predacons. You never know if he'll viciously attack with his power staff or just sweep you off your feet with his massive wings. He may be loyal, but his fierce unpredictability makes him an enemy not to be trifled with.

Checklist

AUTOBOTS

- ☐ Windcharger
- ☐ Trailcutter
- ☐ Optimus Prime
- ☐ Bumblebee
- ☐ Ratchet
- ☐ Arcee
- ☐ Bumblebee

DECEPTICON

☐ Shockwave

PREDACON

☐ Ripclaw

CUSTOM KREONS: 2013 FIGURES

Some KREON Transformers have the rare ability to customize their appearance by mixing and matching select body parts as well as sharing weapons. These upgrades allow them to not only change their form but also enhance their abilities and get brand-new skills in the process.

Optimus Prime

IN: A5413   PN: CUSTOM KREON OPTIMUS PRIME   PC: 41

ALLIANCE: Autobot

STRENGTH: Leadership

BIO: Optimus Prime forged his mighty Beast Blade to help his fellow Autobots fend off the dangerous Predacons. Of course, at his age he'd rather be kicking his thrusters up, but *somebody*'s got to be an awesome leader, right?

Alternate Modes

Bumblebee

IN: A5413   PN: CUSTOM KREON BUMBLEBEE   PC: 40

ALLIANCE: Autobot

STRENGTH: Combat

BIO: Optimus Prime knows the key to keeping Bumblebee from getting into trouble is keeping him busy with as many missions as possible. The Predacons better run for cover, because it's *on*.

Alternate Modes

Ironhide

IN: **A5413**   PN: **CUSTOM KREON IRONHIDE**   PC: **38**

ALLIANCE: Autobot

STRENGTH: Patrolling

BIO: Ironhide has been fighting Decepticons for so long that he remembers when Starscream was in little robot diapers. Or at least that's what he *says*. He loves to tell stories about the past, but no one knows whether they're true. That's how *old* he is! Only his buddy Optimus Prime knows the truth, and he's not talkin'.

Alternate Modes

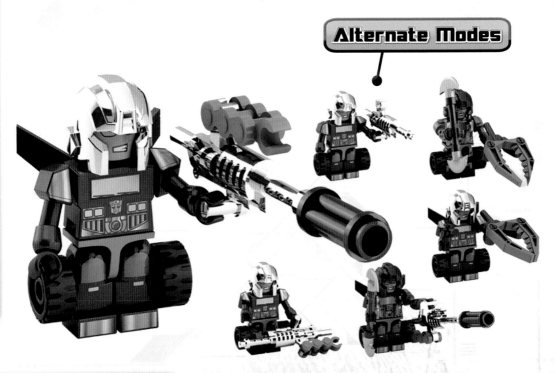

Megatron

IN: **A5413**   PN: **CUSTOM KREON MEGATRON**   PC: **36**

ALLIANCE: Decepticon

STRENGTH: Subjugation

BIO: Megatron finally has more time to read his favorite book now that the Predacons have taken center stage in the battle with the Autobots. And he can start taking those woodworking classes he saw in a magazine. Fun, fun, fun!

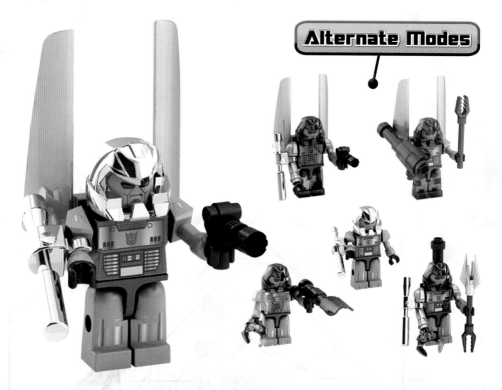

Alternate Modes

71

Soundwave

IN: A5413   PN: CUSTOM KREON SOUNDWAVE   PC: 36

ALLIANCE: Decepticon

STRENGTH: Communications

BIO: Soundwave believes his intelligence-gathering talents are vastly superior to those of his fellow Decepticons. His enemies, however, will tell you he's just a gossipy prude. Whatever! He puts on his headphones and tunes out the haters.

Alternate Modes

Starscream

IN: A5413   **PN:** CUSTOM KREON STARSCREAM   **PC:** 43

ALLIANCE: Decepticon

STRENGTH: Aerial assault

BIO: Starscream is a world-class mischief maker. And he can bowl like you wouldn't believe. Sadly, no one has ever taken the time to get to know that side of him. Time to update his BotBook profile!

Alternate Modes

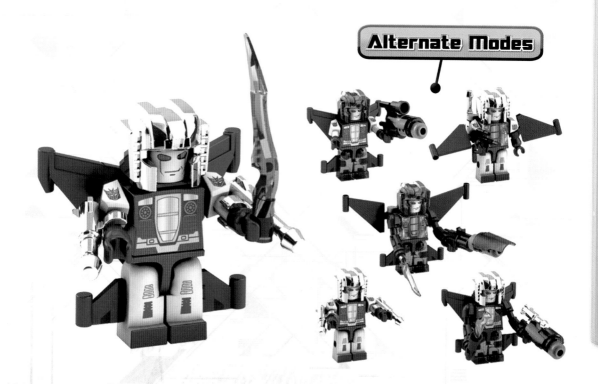

Checklist

AUTOBOTS

- ☐ **Optimus Prime**
- ☐ **Bumblebee**
- ☐ **Ironhide**

DECEPTICONS

☐ **Megatron**

☐ **Soundwave**

☐ **Starscream**

MICRO-CHANGERS: 2012 FIGURES

The war between the Autobots and the Decepticons plateaued over time—until a brand-new threat began appearing that would turn the tide of battle. These advanced KREONS developed the ability to transform themselves, becoming sensational new creations called Micro-Changers. In some cases, they can even join together to build a larger robotic form called a Combiner. With their ranks growing larger, it seems the Autobots and Decepticons may be locked in battle for a very long time.

Crankstart

IN: A2034   PN: MICRO-CHANGER   PC: N/A

ALLIANCE: Decepticon

STRENGTH: Espionage

BIO: Crankstart likes to stay under the radar so he doesn't get teased by his fellow Decepticons. They can be real meanies. Thankfully, staying hidden and fading into the background is his specialty.

Galvatron

IN: A2034 PN: MICRO-CHANGER PC: N/A

ALLIANCE: Decepticon

STRENGTH: Conquering

BIO: Galvatron will tell you himself how awesomely evil he is. This egotistic and unbearable Decepticon won't stop till he rules *everything*. And don't even think about betraying him, because he can sniff out a traitor from a mile away.

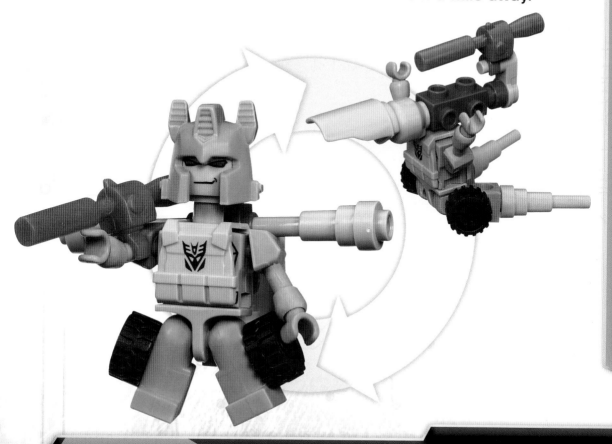

Spinister

IN: **A2034**   PN: **MICRO-CHANGER**   PC: **N/A**

ALLIANCE: Decepticon

STRENGTH: Explosives

BIO: Spinister is always up to something ominous and secretive. He can be *really moody*, too. When he's not blowing up Autobots with his beam cannon, you might catch him reading his favorite novel, *Botlight*. It's a real page-turner.

Sunstorm

IN: A2034 PN: MICRO-CHANGER PC: N/A

ALLIANCE: Decepticon

STRENGTH: Incinerating

BIO: Not only is Sunstorm's body hot to the touch, but he's got a blazing temper to match. Maybe it's because he's always leaking smelly toxic gases from his body. *That* could turn anyone into a hothead.

Scorponok

IN: A2034   PN: MICRO-CHANGER   PC: N/A

ALLIANCE: Predacon

STRENGTH: Assassination

BIO: Scorponok may seem like the perfect warrior, but it's all an act. He's just waiting patiently for the right time to seize the reins of leadership from Galvatron and lead his minions to victory. It's only a matter of time before *everyone* feels Scorponok's sting!

Waspinator

IN: **A2034**   PN: **MICRO-CHANGER**   PC: **N/A**

ALLIANCE: Predacon

STRENGTH: Scheming

BIO: As the Predacons' most gung ho warrior, Waspinator is always ready to sting the Autobots where it hurts. He's suffered a lot of damage in battle and prides himself on wearing his dents and dings like little badges of courage.

Springer

IN: A2200 (WAVE 1)   PN: MICRO-CHANGER   PC: N/A

ALLIANCE: Autobot

STRENGTH: Covert operations

BIO: When Optimus Prime needs a skilled explosives expert for a secret mission, there's only one guy he calls: Springer. Springer occasionally hangs out with his Autobot buddies, but his lack of social skills can make it difficult for him to fit in. And he's got a *super weird* sense of humor. Don't let him tell you the joke about the screwdriver and the lug nut. It's *terrible*.

Singe

IN: A2200 (WAVE 1)   **PN:** MICRO-CHANGER   **PC:** N/A

ALLIANCE: Autobot

STRENGTH: Pyrotechnics

BIO: Singe is mesmerized by an open flame and will show up at a barbecue at the drop of a hat, even if he wasn't invited. He loves watching stuff burn, especially hot dogs, which he will only eat if they're completely black. It's pretty gross.

Quickslinger

IN: A2200 (WAVE 1)   **PN:** MICRO-CHANGER   **PC:** N/A

ALLIANCE: Autobot

STRENGTH: Raiding

BIO: Good things come in small packages! At least that's what Quickslinger keeps telling himself. He might be swift and sleek, but he still gets picked on by his Autobot pals for being a small fry. They certainly don't laugh when he whips out his Deconstructo Blaster, though. *That* thing means business!

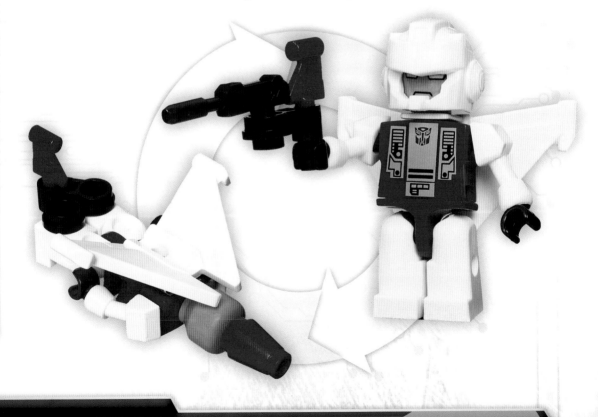

Warpath

IN: A2200 (WAVE 1)   **PN:** MICRO-CHANGER   **PC:** N/A

ALLIANCE: Autobot

STRENGTH: Explosives

BIO: It's no surprise that the Autobots' resident bomb maker is a big fan of fireworks. The lights, the big bangs, and the colors—Warpath loves it all! But what would be even *cooler*? How about watching a bunch of evil Decepticons explode? Now *that*'s some real fun. At least Warpath thinks so.

Blast Off

IN: **A2200 (WAVE 1)**   PN: **MICRO-CHANGER**   PC: **N/A**

ALLIANCE: Decepticon

STRENGTH: Interstellar traveling

BIO: Whenever the pressures of spreading terror are too much for Blast Off to handle, he simply runs away to deep space, where he can clear his head. Flying high above Earth is also a great way to target his enemies so they never see him coming.

Bludgeon

IN: **A2200 (WAVE 1)** PN: **MICRO-CHANGER** PC: **N/A**

ALLIANCE: Decepticon

STRENGTH: Martial arts

BIO: Bludgeon is a bloodthirsty fighter who uses the ancient Cybertronian martial art of Metallikato to subdue his enemies. He's also proficient in Brickshindo but dishonors its peaceful nature by using it for evil. And if none of that works, he has a big energo-sword that's *perfect* for chopping up Autobots.

Hook

IN: A2200 (WAVE 1)   **PN:** MICRO-CHANGER   **PC:** N/A

ALLIANCE: Decepticon

STRENGTH: Architecture

BIO: Hook is a scrappy little brawler who challenges *any* Decepticon to build stuff better than he does. Even though he's angry that he wasn't asked to be a part of Devastator, he's pretty proud that he built the Kreonsler Building.

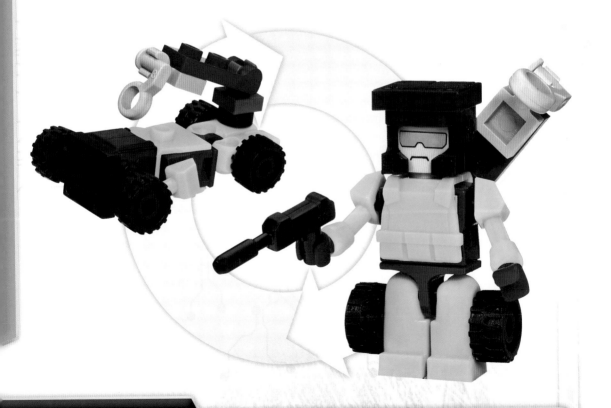

Airachnid

IN: A2200 (WAVE 1)　PN: MICRO-CHANGER　PC: N/A

ALLIANCE: Predacon

STRENGTH: Torture

BIO: Airachnid is a merciless and wicked Decepticon who delights in the torment of her Autobot enemies. She especially loves tickling Arcee till she can't stand it any longer. Airachnid has a large collection of souvenirs from battle and hopes to one day be featured in *Decepticon Home Magazine*.

Insecticon

IN: **A2200 (WAVE 1)**   PN: **MICRO-CHANGER**   PC: **N/A**

ALLIANCE: Predacon

STRENGTH: Surveillance

BIO: Insecticon is always hungry for battle and will chow down on anything and everything in his path. He will go to great lengths for a bite of Autobot hide. Insecticon may not be a bright guy, but his Hydraulic Kick will flatten his enemies in a second.

Inferno

IN: **A2200 (WAVE 1)**   PN: **MICRO-CHANGER**   PC: **N/A**

ALLIANCE: Predacon

STRENGTH: Firefighting

BIO: Inferno is the Predacons' go-to guy when things get a little hot under the collar. One blast of his special fire-suppressing foam and blazes are ended in seconds. And if there's extra foam left over, it can be kind of fun—like a bubble bath!

Rampage

IN: A2200 (WAVE 1)   **PN:** MICRO-CHANGER   **PC:** N/A

ALLIANCE: Predacon

STRENGTH: Smashing

BIO: Don't mess with Rampage. He's got a really short temper and will attack anyone he doesn't like. Oh, and don't even think about taking a sip out of his Energon when he's not looking because he will *crush you*.

Dirge

IN: A2200 (WAVE 1)   **PN: MICRO-CHANGER**   **PC: N/A**

ALLIANCE: Predacon

STRENGTH: Hovering

BIO: If you're looking for a good time, make sure you don't hang out with Dirge. He's always depressed about *something* and can be a real downer. Mostly he feels betrayed by his Predacon pals, but betrayal is kind of their thing!

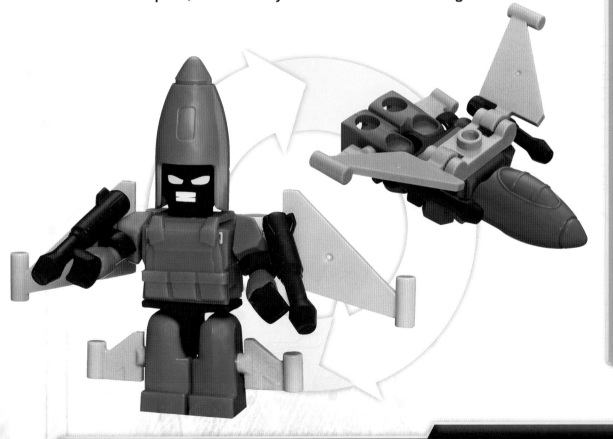

Bulkhead

IN: **A2200 (WAVE 2)**   PN: **MICRO-CHANGER**   PC: **N/A**

ALLIANCE: Autobot

STRENGTH: Sturdiness

BIO: Bulkhead is a big bot with a heart of gold. He can be a fierce warrior when he wants to be, but off the battlefield he wouldn't hurt a butterfly. He actually collects them. Optimus Prime considers Bulkhead a positive role model for the younger Autobots.

Groove

IN: A2200 (WAVE 2)   **PN:** MICRO-CHANGER   **PC:** N/A

ALLIANCE: Autobot

STRENGTH: Peacekeeping

BIO: Groove avoids conflict *as much as possible*. Instead of living life on the edge, he likes to live it in a hammock. Groove plays by his own set of rules, and when the going gets tough, he falls asleep.

Arcee

IN: **A2200 (WAVE 2)**   PN: **MICRO-CHANGER**   PC: **N/A**

ALLIANCE: Autobot

STRENGTH: Sharpshooting

BIO: Arcee loves when Decepticons underestimate her exceptional combat skills. It just makes it easier for her to capture them! She's got a fierce rivalry going with Airachnid, but Arcee's *biggest* weakness is that she really hates to be tickled.

IN: A2200 (WAVE 2) PN: MICRO-CHANGER PC: N/A

ALLIANCE: Autobot

STRENGTH: Aerial acrobatics

BIO: If there isn't an audience around, Powerglide isn't interested. He can *always* streak across the sky like a bolt of lightning, but if nobody's watching, then what's the point? He's a risk taker and a show-off, but his biggest dream is to be on his favorite television show, *KREONS Have Talent*!

Perceptor

IN: A2200 (WAVE 2)   PN: MICRO-CHANGER   PC: N/A

ALLIANCE: Autobot

STRENGTH: Scientific prowess

BIO: On the outside, Perceptor may seem like a stuffy know-it-all, but the truth is that he's just too smart for everyone else. His Autobot buddies may roll their eyes when he starts using all that scientific jibber-jabber, but deep down they know how hard he works to help the team when he's off the battlefield.

Hoist

IN: A2200 (WAVE 2)   **PN: MICRO-CHANGER**   **PC: N/A**

ALLIANCE: Autobot

STRENGTH: Surgery

BIO: You'd think an Autobot would look *forward* to getting medical attention after an injury on the battlefield, but when Hoist is the bot patching you up, it becomes a different story. Sure he's nice, but his jokes are the worst! It's a small price to pay for good service, though.

Guzzle

IN: **A2200 (WAVE 2)**   PN: **MICRO-CHANGER**   PC: **N/A**

ALLIANCE: Autobot

STRENGTH: Obeying orders

BIO: Guzzle has a constant craving for Energon and isn't afraid to mooch some from his Autobot pals when his supply runs out. It makes sense, seeing that he's always working out. This bot is *a machine*! It takes a lot of work to look this good.

Huffer

IN: A2200 (WAVE 2)   **PN: MICRO-CHANGER**   **PC: N/A**

ALLIANCE: Autobot

STRENGTH: Engineering

BIO: While the other Autobots enjoy their time on Earth, Huffer feels trapped and would rather be back on Cybertron. He's constantly complaining about one thing or another, and it drives his friends bonkers. He doesn't get out to exercise much, unless you count *eye rolls* as exercise.

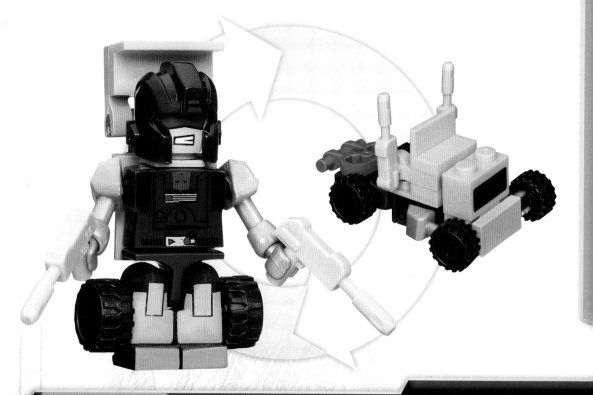

Bolt

IN: **A2200 (WAVE 2)**   PN: **MICRO-CHANGER**   PC: **N/A**

ALLIANCE: Decepticon

STRENGTH: Wrecking

BIO: Bolt is a dangerous force, not because he's a tough-as-nails fighting machine but because he smells absolutely *horrible*. Enemies take cover because they can smell him coming from a mile away. His friends have tried to get him to the car wash, but he says the spritz tickles him too much.

Bombshell

IN: A2200 (WAVE 2)   PN: MICRO-CHANGER   PC: N/A

ALLIANCE: Decepticon

STRENGTH: Manipulation

BIO: Bombshell plays with his victims as if they are toys. Watching his enemies break down brings him great happiness. Needless to say, he wasn't voted Sweetest at the KREON King Pageant this year.

Scourge

IN: A2200 (WAVE 2)   **PN:** MICRO-CHANGER   **PC:** N/A

ALLIANCE: Decepticon

STRENGTH: Tracking

BIO: Scourge is definitely getting to be too old to be zooming around the skies looking for fights. When he's not complaining about his sore thrusters, he's yelling about how all these new Decepticons have no respect for the old days. But he does have one redeeming quality: the sweetest KREON mustache ever!

Vehicon

IN: A2200 (WAVE 2)   **PN:** MICRO-CHANGER   **PC:** N/A

ALLIANCE: Decepticon

STRENGTH: Compliance

BIO: If there were an award for sucking up, Vehicon would win it every single time. He's always showering Megatron with compliments and praise, while talking badly about the leader behind his back. It's really not cool—and dangerous to boot. One bad move, and Vehicon could be headed to the trash heap!

Lugnut

IN: A2200 (WAVE 2) **PN:** MICRO-CHANGER **PC:** N/A

ALLIANCE: Decepticon

STRENGTH: Tactics

BIO: What Lugnut lacks in simple smarts, he more than makes up for in brawn. He's extremely loyal to Megatron, who often takes advantage of Lugnut by constantly playing pranks on him. Lugnut just smiles and nods like a poor little blockhead.

Acidwing

IN: **A2200 (WAVE 2)**   PN: **MICRO-CHANGER**   PC: **N/A**

ALLIANCE: Predacon

STRENGTH: Diving attacks

BIO: With a bright green body, Acidwing has a hard time blending in with his Predacon colleagues. He stands out *so much* it makes him an easy target. It's a small price to pay for looking good.

Beachcomber

IN: A2200 (WAVE 3)   **PN:** MICRO-CHANGER   **PC:** N/A

ALLIANCE: Autobot

STRENGTH: Free-wheeling

BIO: Beachcomber's motto is "Dude, chill!" As the Autobots' resident wanderer, he hopes that one day his colleagues will be able to put aside their differences with the Decepticons and move forward peacefully. Beachcomber may be a peaceful guy, but he's also a stinky one.

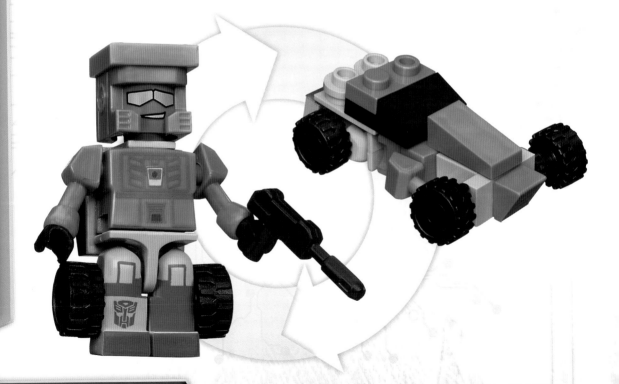

Cheetor

IN: A2200 (WAVE 3)   PN: **MICRO-CHANGER**   PC: **N/A**

ALLIANCE: Autobot

STRENGTH: Agility

BIO: Cheetor loves the thrill of the hunt, and when Decepticons are on the loose, he's the first guy in line to chase them down. He might be quick on his feet but always makes sure to *think* before he acts. On the weekends, Cheetor loves finding funky animal-print stuff for his jungle-themed living quarters.

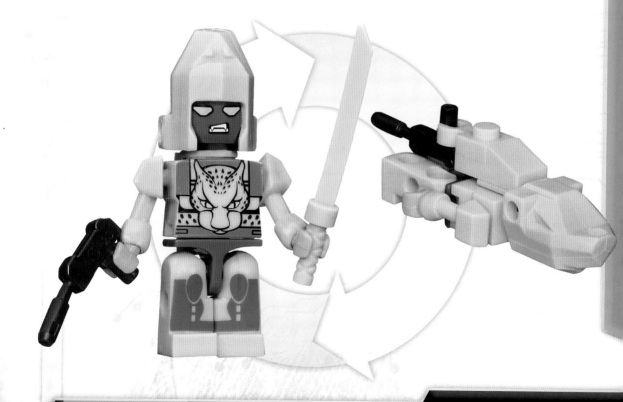

Seawing

IN: A2200 (WAVE 3) **PN:** MICRO-CHANGER **PC:** N/A

ALLIANCE: Autobot

STRENGTH: Aquatics

BIO: Autobots love being the center of attention, but Seawing likes submerging himself deep in the ocean, where he can think without a bunch of distractions. He's not a fan of bright lights, so keep those headlights off. And no littering, either. That's totally not cool.

Nosecone

IN: A2200 (WAVE 3) PN: MICRO-CHANGER PC: N/A

ALLIANCE: Autobot

STRENGTH: Tinkering

BIO: Nosecone is a careful perfectionist who takes the time to do things correctly rather than risk messing them up. He is very proud of his role as the Autobots' resident tinkerer, but do *not* throw him a surprise birthday party. He *hates* surprises.

Kickback

IN: **A2200 (WAVE 3)**   PN: **MICRO-CHANGER**   PC: **N/A**

ALLIANCE: Decepticon

STRENGTH: Conspiring

BIO: Kickback is a master manipulator who will be sweet and nice to his friends' faces while bad-mouthing and betraying them behind their backs. He has no remorse for his actions and enjoys making his weaker colleagues do his dirty work.

Longhaul

IN: A2200 (WAVE 3) **PN: MICRO-CHANGER** **PC: N/A**

ALLIANCE: Decepticon

STRENGTH: Obeying orders

BIO: None of the Decepticons treat Longhaul with the respect he thinks he deserves. So what does he do about it? *Nothing.* He's too tired from lugging around weapons all day. He longs for battle! He dreams of excitement! He thirsts for danger! But also his back hurts and he's *exhausted.*

Nemesis Prime

IN: A2200 (WAVE 3)   **PN:** MICRO-CHANGER   **PC:** N/A

ALLIANCE: Decepticon

STRENGTH: Ruthlessness

BIO: Nemesis Prime is exactly like Optimus Prime, except without all the nice stuff. They're both cunning, strong, intelligent, and powerful. But whereas Optimus is a benevolent leader, Nemesis lacks a code of ethics, which makes him merciless and cutthroat.

Thrust

IN: A2200 (WAVE 3)   PN: MICRO-CHANGER   PC: N/A

ALLIANCE: Decepticon

STRENGTH: Babbling

BIO: Thrust thinks he's got major swag going on, but the truth is he has a big ego and thinks his fuel pipe doesn't stink. He is just jealous of his fellow Decepticons because they get more credit than he does.

Ramjet

IN: A2200 (WAVE 3) **PN:** MICRO-CHANGER **PC:** N/A

ALLIANCE: Decepticon

STRENGTH: Zooming

BIO: Ramjet is a stubborn Decepticon who doesn't care what you think of his actions. He's been hit in the head so many times in battle that it's left him a little loopy and forgetful.

Sharkticon

IN: A2200 (WAVE 3) **PN:** MICRO-CHANGER **PC:** N/A

ALLIANCE: Decepticon

STRENGTH: Malevolence

BIO: Sharkticon is a ferocious underwater predator who's hungry for carnage morning, noon, and night. He's obedient to a fault and usually jumps into combat before thinking. The worst thing of all is that Sharkticon is a biter. And *no one* likes a biter.

Checklist

PREVIEW WAVE DECEPTICONS

- ☐ **Crankstart**
- ☐ **Galvatron**
- ☐ **Spinister**
- ☐ **Sunstorm**

PREVIEW WAVE PREDACONS

- ☐ **Scorponok**
- ☐ **Waspinator**

WAVE 1 AUTOBOTS

- ☐ **Springer**
- ☐ **Singe**
- ☐ **Quickslinger**
- ☐ **Warpath**

WAVE 1 DECEPTICONS

- ☐ **Blast Off**
- ☐ **Bludgeon**
- ☐ **Hook**

WAVE 1 PREDACONS

- ☐ **Airachnid**
- ☐ **Insecticon**
- ☐ **Inferno**
- ☐ **Rampage**
- ☐ **Dirge**

WAVE 2 AUTOBOTS

- ☐ Bulkhead
- ☐ Groove
- ☐ Arcee
- ☐ Powerglide
- ☐ Perceptor
- ☐ Hoist
- ☐ Guzzle
- ☐ Huffer

WAVE 2 DECEPTICONS

- ☐ Bolt
- ☐ Bombshell
- ☐ Scourge
- ☐ Vehicon
- ☐ Lugnut

WAVE 2 PREDACON

- ☐ Acidwing

WAVE 3 AUTOBOTS

- ☐ Beachcomber
- ☐ Cheetor
- ☐ Seawing
- ☐ Nosecone

WAVE 3 DECEPTICONS

- ☐ Kickback
- ☐ Longhaul
- ☐ Nemesis Prime
- ☐ Thrust
- ☐ Ramjet
- ☐ Sharkticon

MICRO-CHANGER COMBINERS: 2013 FIGURES

Micro-Changer Combiners have the ability to transform and assemble themselves into larger, more dynamic robot forms. They are known for their versatility in battle since they can often be powerful weapons or sleek vehicles. Micro-Changer Combiners may not seem impressive but are considered extremely dangerous.

123

Superion

IN: A2204 (WAVE 1)   **PN:** SUPERION   **PC:** 76

ALLIANCE: Autobot

MEMBERS: Air Raid, Firestrike, Silverbolt, Skydive

STRENGTH: Aerial strikes

BIO: Superion definitely lives up to his name as an exceptional and committed Autobot combiner. When assembled, the members of the team work together to solve the problem at hand. Even though he can be a bit of a braggart, Superion's collaborative spirit inspires his fellow Autobots. He's also been voted Sleekest by *Bot Style Magazine* so, yeah, you can be jealous now.

Air Raid

Silverbolt

Firestrike

Skydive

Bruticus

IN: A2204 (WAVE 1) PN: BRUTICUS PC: 79

ALLIANCE: Decepticon

MEMBERS: Brawl, Onslaught, Swindle, Vortex

STRENGTH: Tyranny

BIO: Bruticus knows that he's not the smartest bot in the world, but he makes up for it by being super strong and brutish. Bruticus is also obsessively jealous of Superion's ability to fly. Some might say he has a *Superion complex*. In the meantime, he's perfectly happy just stomping everyone into the ground.

Brawl

Swindle

Onslaught

Vortex

Devastator

IN: A2204 (WAVE 1)   PN: DEVASTATOR   PC: 77

ALLIANCE: Decepticon

MEMBERS: Bonecrusher, Mixmaster, Scavenger, Scrapper

STRENGTH: Ravaging

BIO: Devastator craves Energon. He *lives* for it. It's all he thinks about sometimes. There are even times in battle where he'll grow tired and simply run away in search of some of that sweet stuff. When he's focused, however, he can be a real king of carnage.

Bonecrusher

Scavenger

Mixmaster

Scrapper

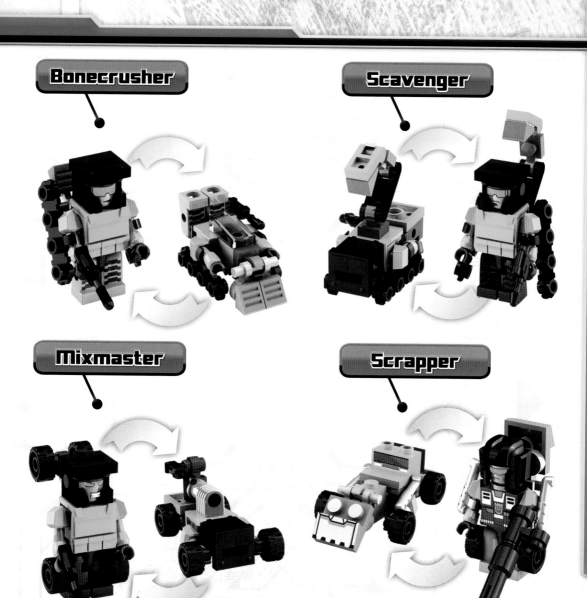

Predaking

IN: A2204 (WAVE 1)   PN: PREDAKING   PC: 80

ALLIANCE: Predacon

MEMBERS: Divebomb, Headlock, Razorclaw, Torox

STRENGTH: Fierceness

BIO: Predaking is a primal beast who relishes the opportunity to torture his Autobot victims once he has ambushed and caught them. He can be vicious on the battlefield, but in private he keeps a very emotional journal.

Divebomb

Razorclaw

Headlock

Torox

Defensor

IN: **A2204 (WAVE 2)**   PN: **DEFENSOR**   PC: **85**

ALLIANCE: Autobot

MEMBERS: Blades, First Aid, Hot Spot, Streetsmart

STRENGTH: Security

BIO: Human life is a precious thing. That's why Defensor is so committed to protecting humans from danger. Humans look up to him as their guardian and admire his bravery and courage. In his combined form, the members work as one. He's considered a hero by many, but to him he's just doing his job.

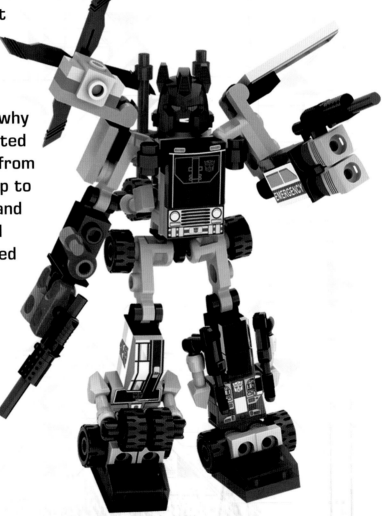

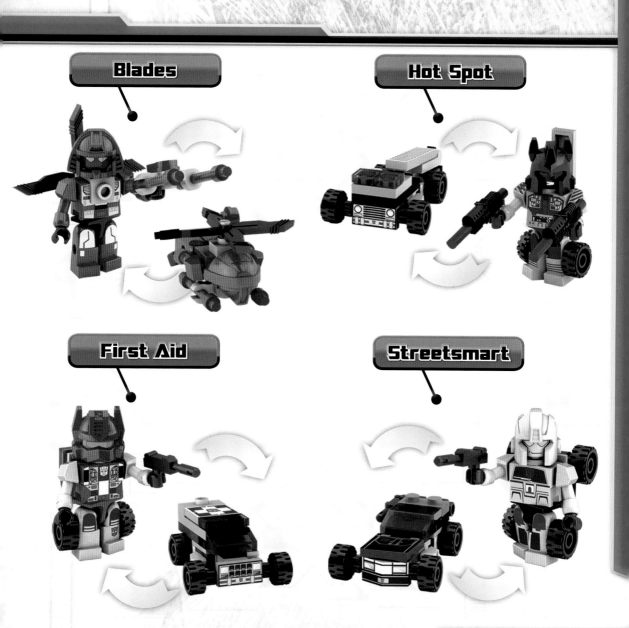

Blades

Hot Spot

First Aid

Streetsmart

Piranacon

IN: A2204 (WAVE 2)   PN: PIRANACON   PC: 95

ALLIANCE: Decepticon

MEMBERS: Nautilator, Overbite, Snaptrap, Tentakill

STRENGTH: Hunting

BIO: Piranacon won't stop until he's caught his prey. If that means chasing Autobots all day long, so be it. He's *that* committed to the cause of evil and destruction. His extreme dedication exhausts his fellow Decepticons, who consider him a mere flunky who kisses up to the boss to look good.

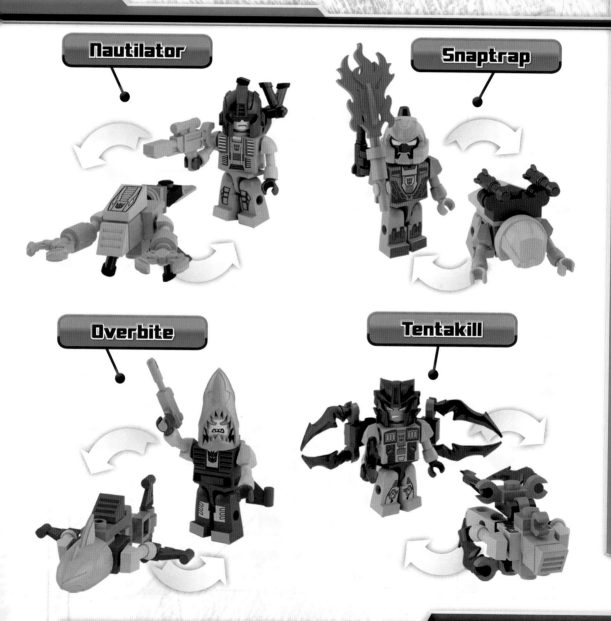

Nautilator

Snaptrap

Overbite

Tentakill

Abominus

IN: A2204 (WAVE 2)   PN: ABOMINUS   PC: 85

ALLIANCE: Decepticon

MEMBERS: Hun Gur, Rippersnapper, Sinnertwin, Windrazor

STRENGTH: Terror

BIO: Abominus is a rage-filled beast who doesn't understand simple commands when in his combined form. The Decepticons basically just point him in the right direction and watch him wreak havoc on whatever might be in his path. His limited intelligence makes it difficult for him to communicate. He's tried taking anger management classes, but he usually just smashes the coffee machine to pieces and then leaves.

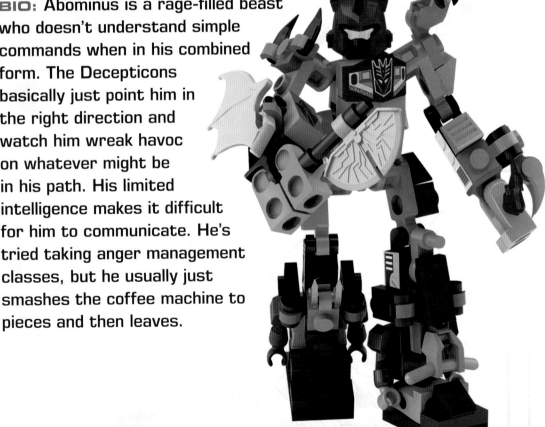

Hun Gur

Sinnertwin

Rippersnapper

Windrazor

Checklist

WAVE 1 AUTOBOT

☐ Superion

WAVE 1 DECEPTICONS

☐ Bruticus

☐ Devastator

WAVE 1 PREDACON

☐ Predaking

WAVE 2 AUTOBOT

☐ Defensor

WAVE 2 DECEPTICONS

☐ Piranacon

☐ Abominus

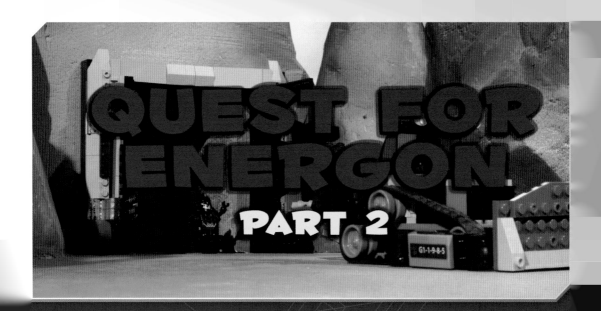

QUEST FOR ENERGON

PART 2

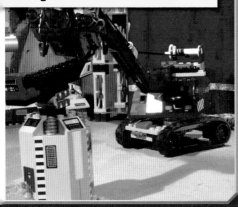

Megatron uses the stolen Energon to build a new device.

The device makes grilled cheese sandwiches.

Autobots in disguise...

...go into the Decepticon camp to distract them.

HUH?

I ♥ GRILLED CHEESE

The forecast says CHEESE!

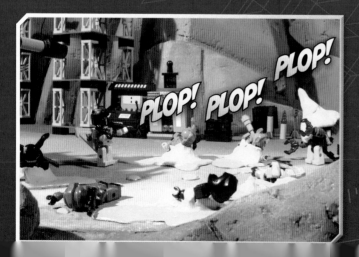

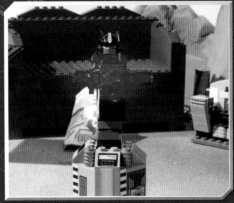

The Autobots saved the Energon!